To Martín, my brother from another mother, who inspires me to be kind.
— R.D.

To my mum and dad for all their support, interest, and kindness.
— S.J.

Copyright © 2015 by March 4th, Inc.
Cover and internal design © 2017 by Sourcebooks, Inc.
Text by Rana DiOrio
Illustrated by Stéphane Jorisch

Sourcebooks and the colophon are registered trademarks of Sourcebooks, Inc.

Published by Little Pickle Press, an imprint of Sourcebooks Jabberwocky.
P.O. Box 4410, Naperville, Illinois 60567-4410
(630) 961-3900
Fax: (630) 961-2168
sourcebooks.com

Library of Congress Cataloging-in-Publication Data is on file with the publisher.

Source of Production: Worzalla, Stevens Point, Wisconsin, USA
Date of Production: July 2017
Run Number: 5010002

Printed and bound in the United States of America.
WOZ 10 9 8 7 6 5 4 3

What Does It Mean to Be Kind?

by Rana DiOrio

Illustrated by Stéphane Jorisch

Little Pickle Press

What does it mean to be kind?

Does it mean trying
to please others?
No.

Does it mean giving gifts expecting something in return? No.

Does it mean pretending you like something you don't? No!

Being kind means...

...smiling at the new student in class.

...giving someone a sincere compliment.

...holding the door open for someone else.

...sticking up for someone who is being bullied.

...seeing the best in people even when they are struggling to be their best.

...forgiving someone who has hurt you.

...helping an injured
or lost animal.

school Play → tickets

...being patient even when you are in a hurry.

...saying "please" and "thank you,"

"you're welcome" and "I'm sorry."

...celebrating differences in others.

...encouraging someone who needs support.

...picking up trash that isn't yours.

...allowing yourself to make
mistakes and to learn from them.

...noticing when someone is sad and
taking the time to understand why.

...caring for those less fortunate than you are.

Being kind means having the courage

to treat others the way you like to be treated.

So show your friends what it means to be kind.

And spread the word—
    if we can all be kind to each other and to ourselves,
    our world will be more loving, caring, and harmonious.

Little Pickle Press
Environmental Benefits Statement

This book is printed on Reincarnation Matte Paper. It is made with 100% PCRF (Post-Consumer Recovered Fiber) and Green Power. It is FSC®-certified, acid-free, and ECF (Elemental Chlorine-Free). All of the electricity required to manufacture the paper used to print this book is matched with RECS (Renewable Energy Credits) from Green-e® certified energy sources, primarily wind.

Little Pickle Press saved the following resources by using Reincarnation paper:

trees	energy	greenhouse gases	wastewater	solid waste
Post-consumer recovered fiber displaces wood fiber with savings translated as trees.	PCRF content displaces energy used to process equivalent virgin fiber.	Measured in CO_2 equivalents, PCRF content and Green Power reduce greenhouse gas emissions.	PCRF content eliminates wastewater needed to process equivalent virgin fiber.	PCRF content eliminates solid waste generated by producing an equivalent amount of virgin fiber through the pulp and paper manufacturing process.
13 trees	**5 mil BTUs**	**1,120 lbs**	**6,076 gal**	**406 lbs**

Environmental impacts estimates were made using the Environmental Paper Network Calculator Version 3.2 and applies to a print quantity of 2,000 books. For more information visit www.papercalculator.org.

Kindness

Every act of kindness is also an act of courage. Small gestures can make a big difference to other people, animals, the planet, and even to yourself! There are many different ways you can be kind. Before you try an activity, try answering these questions to help you think about the meaning of kindness:

- Why is it important to be a kind person?
- How can we show kindness and respect for other people?
- How can we show kindness and respect for ourselves?
- How are you kind to others?
- How does it make you feel to be kind?

What You Can Do

Kindness can be contagious. Making a choice to be kind to others, including animals and the planet, can have a ripple effect that can positively change the world. Here are a few things you can try (remember to ask a caring adult for permission and assistance with big acts of kindness):

- Create a kindness poster to hang in your home or at school.
- Create a "bucket of kindness."
  1. You will need: paper, scissors, a pen or markers, and a clean bucket or large bowl or jar
  2. Cut the paper into strips (any size you'd like)
  3. Write kind messages about friendship or family on the slips of paper.
  4. Ask your friends or family to write messages too.
  5. Fold the slips of paper and add them all to the Bucket of Kindness
  6. When someone needs a positive message, they can reach into the bucket and pull out some instant words of kindness!

- Volunteer at a local shelter or food bank.
- Talk to someone at school who looks like they need a friend.
- Volunteer to help clean up debris or garbage from your neighborhood, a park, or a forest preserve.
- Start a collection of food and animal needs to donate to an animal shelter. (Be sure to check with the shelter's wish list before collecting any items.)
- Plan a kindness day at home or at school.

These are just a few examples of ways to spread kindness. Talk with your friends, family, and teachers to create an even bigger list of ideas. What would happen if you tried to do at least one kind idea every day? You have the power to make good choices, be selfless, have empathy, and respect yourself and others. Be kind!

For more information, including lesson plans, please visit LittlePicklePress.com

littlepicklepress.com

About the Author

Rana DiOrio aspires to be kind each and every day. She believes the single most important value she can teach her children is to be kind. To her, being kind is about following The Golden Rule—that is, treating others the way you would like to be treated. Rana and her children practice random acts of kindness at home and reward one another with "kind karma" points. According to Rana, positively reinforcing and celebrating kindness feels resonant and inspires further kind acts.

Rana has written her way through life—as a student, lawyer, investment banker, investor, and now as an author and entrepreneur. Her interests include fitness training, practicing yoga, reading non-fiction and children's books, dreaming, effecting positive change in the world, and, of course, being global, green, present, safe, kind, entrepreneurial, and American. She lives in San Francisco, California, with The Cowboy and her three children. Follow Rana DiOrio on Twitter @ranadiorio.

About the Illustrator

Stéphane Jorisch was born in Brussels, Belgium, and grew up in Lachine, Quebec, where his father, an illustrator of European comic strips, introduced him to illustrative art at a young age. Jorisch, whose illustration work is most often produced in water-color, gouache, and pen and ink, has won many awards, including the prestigious Canadian Governor General's Award for Children's Illustration and the Toronto Dominion Canadian Children's Literature Award. The illustrator of over eighty books for Canadian, European, and US publishers, some of his recent titles include *New Year at the Pier* by April Halprin Wayland, the Betty Bunny series by Michael B. Kaplan, and *My Father Knows the Names of Things* by Jane Yolen. In addition to his work for young readers, Stéphane Jorisch also illustrates for magazines and has created designs for the renowned Cirque du Soleil. He lives in Montreal with his wife and their three children.